Stop Living Paycheck to Paycheck: The Six Secrets to Becoming Wealthy

Six common sense and powerful money management secrets that can help you escape living paycheck to paycheck and put you on the path to building real wealth.

By Larry Darter

Copyright © 2016 by Larry Darter

Tin Cup Media Press

All rights reserved. No part of this publication may be reproduced in any form, or by any means, electronic, mechanical, or otherwise without the expressed consent in writing of the copyright holder except for the inclusion of quotations in a review.

Although the author has thoroughly researched all sources to ensure the accuracy and completeness of the information presented in this book, we assume no responsibility for inaccuracies, errors, omissions, or inconsistencies contained herein.

No opinions expressed in this book should be construed as a specific inducement to make a particular investment or follow a particular strategy. While opinions expressed in this book by the author are based upon information he considers reliable, the author does not warrant its completeness or accuracy. When it comes to investing, past performance is no guarantee of future results. The author guarantees no specific outcome or profit. The reader must be aware of the real risk of loss in following any investment strategy or investment discussed in this book. The information presented in this book does not take into account the particular investment objectives, financial situation, or needs of any particular person and is not intended as recommendations appropriate to any particular person. Before acting on the information presented in this book the reader should consider whether it is suitable for his or her particular circumstances and should consider seeking advice from his or her own financial or investment advisor.

ISBN-13: 978-1530808182

ISBN-10: 1530808189

For Suzy who teaches me that happiness is the greatest wealth and love the truest riches.

Contents

Foreword

Chapter 1 Understanding the Paycheck to Paycheck Cycle

Chapter 2 First Secret: Start Building Wealth

Chapter 3 Second Secret: Spend Less Than You Earn

Chapter 4 Third Secret: Grow Your Wealth

Chapter 5 Fourth Secret: Protect Your Wealth from Loss

Chapter 6 Fifth Secret: Buying a Home is Still the Best Investment

Chapter 7 Sixth Secret: Assure Your Future Wealth

Chapter 8 Putting It All Together

FOREWORD

Living paycheck to paycheck is an expression that describes a person who would be unable to meet his or her financial obligations if faced with a serious, even short-term significant financial setback. Examples of such financial impediments might be an acute illness or an accident resulting in a short-term disability that prevents a person from being able to work for a significant period of time. Losing a job and being unemployed for an extended period of time would be another example.

Any of those situations I described would be financially challenging for just about anyone, but they would be devastating for someone living paycheck to paycheck. That's because the income of a person living paycheck to paycheck is primarily devoted to expenses. Such a person is quite literally a paycheck or two away from living on the street should his or her paychecks suddenly stop.

The definition of living paycheck to paycheck assumes having limited or no savings to fall back on which puts a person at greater financial risk if suddenly unemployed or unable to work than someone who has accumulated a cushion of savings.

Some might assume that individuals living paycheck to paycheck are what is sometimes referred to as the working poor; people with limited education, limited job skills, and who are predominantly employed in minimum wage jobs. The fact is nothing could be further from the truth. Consider some rather startling facts gleaned from recent studies and surveys that puts a more accurate face on exactly who in America is living paycheck to paycheck.

A 2013 survey by Bankrate.com found that roughly three-quarters of Americans were living paycheck to paycheck.

In 2014, an economic study conducted by researchers at the prestigious Brookings Institution found that more than 25 million middle class American families were living paycheck to paycheck. These were families who had decent jobs with median incomes of $41,000, owned homes, and even had funded retirement accounts.

According to a 2015 survey by SunTrust Bank, one in three people surveyed in households earning more than $75,000 a year said they were living paycheck to paycheck and one in four people in households earning more $100,000 a year said the same thing.

Clearly, as these statistics show, it isn't just the working poor in America who are living paycheck to paycheck. Living hand-to-mouth seems to be a systemic problem that cuts a wide swath across all American socio-economic levels.

A living paycheck to paycheck existence, factually a paycheck or two away from living on the street, is a very risky way to live. But it's not only that. It also robs people of both opportunities and happiness. Let's face it, the more opportunities we have in life, the fuller and more satisfying it becomes. But living paycheck to paycheck serves to severely limit an individual's opportunities and options in so many areas. For example, living paycheck to paycheck can limit a person's job choices, educational choices, the choice of what kind of home to live in, and where he or she can choose to live. It truly affects not just quality of life but every aspect of life, not just a person's financial well-being.

No one really chooses to live paycheck to paycheck. People find themselves in the situation for a number of different reasons. Sometimes individuals and families are forced into it by circumstances beyond their control. Some live paycheck to paycheck because they just never had an opportunity to learn effective money management skills. As a result they may have made some bad financial decisions.

For those living paycheck to paycheck the reasons why aren't important. That is history and as we all well know, there is nothing we can do to change history. What is important for those individuals and families is getting the opportunity to have a better future by improving their financial circumstances so that they can enjoy a richer and fuller life and the chance to start building wealth. That is what this book is about.

The fact that you picked up and are reading this book suggests that you may see yourself as someone who is living paycheck to paycheck. Maybe it always seems there is far too much month left at the end of your paychecks. It also suggests you are tired of living a life where you go to work every day and work hard, but never seem have anything to show for it or never get ahead financially. More importantly your interest in reading this book indicates you are not only looking for a way out from under living paycheck to paycheck but are ready to take action to change your financial circumstances. I believe the information in this book can help you.

This is not a book about another get rich quick scheme. There are enough books like that out there already, masquerading as personal finance advice books. If you were looking for that, you might as well put this book aside now and look for something to read more like *How to Make $1,000,000 as a Day Trader Automatically.*

What you will find in this book are six common sense and realistic tactics you can use to escape the living paycheck to paycheck cycle and start building wealth. I call them the six "secrets" of building wealth, but these six strategies are only secrets in the sense that so many people are oblivious to them.

The six secrets I reveal in this book were not invented by me. I didn't just think them up. Instead I painstakingly discovered them. I uncovered them one by one in various places years ago when I too was caught in the living paycheck to paycheck trap and was searching for a way out. These six principles of wise money management aren't anything new. I truly believe that these secrets are likely as timeless as money itself. I also suspect that they were widely followed by the wise in times past but were somehow lost and forgotten. If anything I simply rediscovered them and perhaps by luck as much as anything, recognized that when you fit these six money management tactics together, they form a powerful, comprehensive, complete, wealth-building personal finance strategy.

When I was stuck living paycheck to paycheck, I didn't necessarily wish to be rich. I just wanted to have enough money so that I didn't have to continually struggle financially. These six secrets accomplished that for me and more. It didn't happen overnight. It required time, it required work, and it required self-discipline because it wasn't always easy to stick to the plan. But I managed to do it and you can too.

Today, some 15 years since I discovered and starting using the six principles this book is about, I consider myself wealthy. I don't struggle financially anymore. In fact, I can pretty much do whatever I want, whenever I want without worrying about money. Don't misunderstand. I can't just buy anything I want. I'm certainly not wealthy in the sense of a Bill Gates or Warren Buffett, the two men who occupy the number one and two positions respectively on the most recent Forbes 400 list of wealthiest Americans. But I am in the position to take advantage of a lot of opportunities in life that are generally beyond the reach of a large percentage of Americans today, those still living paycheck to paycheck. I'll never become a member of the Fortune 400 club, but financially I'm in a very good place right now.

Being wealthy has it perks. If I wished, I could tell my boss tomorrow that I'm taking some time off and could spontaneously take a vacation to virtually anywhere in the world. Best of all I wouldn't have to max out a credit card to do it. I'm not saying I'd be flying first class and drinking champagne or that I'd be staying at a five-star hotel and eating in the most expensive restaurants when I arrived at my chosen destination. But I could easily afford to pay for a spur-of-the-moment vacation without relying on plastic. Wealth allows you to do that sort of thing.

I'm in a good place financially now, but it wasn't always that way. I lived paycheck to paycheck until my mid-forties. It wasn't until then that I began to suspect that it didn't have to be that way, that there was something I could do, something I could learn that could radically change my financial future. That's when I began to read, study, and to search for answers. That's how I discovered the six secrets. That's when I became motivated to act to change my financial circumstances. While I got a relatively late start on building wealth, if I'm fortunate enough to live a full life I fully expect to be a millionaire one day.

If you on the other hand are under the age of 30, which frankly is the demographic that I really aimed to reach with this book when I decided to write it, time and the miracle of compound interest is on your side. With fifteen years or more than I have had to work with, if you learn and put into practice the principles I'm sharing with this book, you will easily amass far more wealth than I ever will.

If you're ready to start learning how to leave living paycheck to paycheck behind for good and are ready to learn how to start building wealth, turn the page and let's get started.

1

Understanding the Paycheck to Paycheck Cycle

You really need to know that it isn't your fault that you have become ensnared in the living paycheck to paycheck rat race. There are good reasons that it happened that had very little to do with you. You aren't a failure or just not smart enough to figure out how to manage your money and build wealth on your own. What it really comes down to is this. You, I, and millions of others were simply never taught how to manage money and money has to be managed if a person is to prosper and attain real wealth.

I know I was never taught any basic money skills. It wasn't taught in the high school I graduated from. In fact, for the most part it still isn't taught in high schools in this country. A recent article published in U.S. News & World Report noted that only 13 of the fifty U.S. states require high school students to take a basic personal finance course to graduate.

Odds are, of the estimated 3 million plus students who graduate from high schools in the United States each year, few of them graduate even knowing how to properly balance a checkbook. I tend to believe that financial illiteracy is one of the principal reasons that so many college seniors are graduating these days with student loan debt loads so high that many of them will still be repaying their own student loans when their children reach college age.

I also didn't learn any basic money lessons from my parents nor did countless others. Our parents can't teach us what they were never taught. My parents are wonderful people whom I love and respect very much, but until well past middle age, they too were caught in the trap of living paycheck to paycheck. They did eventually learn to manage money better but not in time to save much for their retirement years. Like so many other retired Americans they are now largely dependent on social security for their financial support.

While it was not until my mid-forties that I discovered the six secrets of money management this book is about, putting these secrets into practice allowed me to retire more than a decade before I reached the traditional retirement age and qualified to claim social security benefits.

While I was able to retire early with adequate income to meet my living expenses, I hadn't accumulated enough wealth to have the retirement lifestyle I really wanted. For one thing I love to travel abroad. I've seen a good part of the world but there is so much more of it I want to see and experience and that takes money. To do that, four years into retirement I decided to return to work to earn additional income for travel and to pay for other things I enjoy that add to my quality of life.

I plan to continue working, at least part-time until I do reach social security qualifying age. For one thing I found after four years in early retirement that I wasn't really ready to stop working altogether. I also enjoy earning an income once again because it allows me to continue practicing the six secrets and to continue building wealth. As a result, when I do decide to retire for good, I'll be in even better financial shape than when I retired the first time.

The fact that I continue to work is a choice. It doesn't mean the six secrets didn't work. They did and following them radically changed my financial circumstances. I'm still benefitting from that today. But I got a late start which shows the importance of time with respect to building wealth.

When I decided to write this book, my hope was that I could share these six secrets with people in their twenties and thirties. Quite simply the younger you are when you learn and put these secrets to work, the more wealth and prosperity you will enjoy and the sooner you can start reaping the benefits of these powerful money management principles. That said, don't let your age be a barrier to learning and embracing these principles. Whatever age you are, if you are are working and earning income you will benefit from learning and following these secrets to building wealth.

Before we continue to the first of the six secrets, the topic of the very next chapter, let's understand each other. If you are anything like me, you are probably wondering right now whether you can trust me. Is this book legitimate? Are the six secrets to wealth a legitimate financial strategy or is this all something I just made up to sell books? Am I really out to help others escape living paycheck to paycheck or am I just attempting to turn a profit at the expense of others? If I'm such a benevolent soul, why not just put the secrets on the web where people can read the information and learn the principles of wealth building for free instead of having to buy a book?

Those are all fair questions. In fact those are the same kinds of questions I ask myself whenever I pick up a personal finance book. But let me tell you briefly why I decided to write this book and why I decided to write it now some 15 years after discovering and profiting personally from these six secrets.

Let me begin by simply saying in all sincerity that these six principles are legitimate. I know they work because they worked for me and in fact continue to work for me to this very day. I have absolutely no reason to believe they won't work for anyone else willing to learn and follow them.

That said, you don't know me and I certainly do not expect you to trust me on the basis of blind faith. But I am confident that if you read this book from beginning to end, take time to study and learn the principles I'm sharing with you, and more importantly put them into practice, you will arrive at your own informed decision that the principles are legitimate, that they do exactly what I represent they will do.

As I stated in the foreword to the book, this book is not about a get rich quick scheme. The information in this book has in my considered opinion the power to make you wealthy. Alone however, these six secrets will not put you on the Forbes 400 list with the likes of Bill Gates. In addition to learning how to wisely manage his personal finances at some point, Bill Gates also created a computer operating system that has literally dominated the industry for the past three decades. Gates leveraged that achievement into what is estimated to be a $76 billion net worth. The point is, if you aspire to be a multi-billionaire, it will require more than this book or any book to achieve that goal. That being said, if you learn the six principles in this book and apply them, there is no reason why you won't have a net worth measured in millions by the time you reach retirement age. And you will live a life free of money worries in the meanwhile.

I was motivated to write this book and write it now as a result of witnessing the dramatic changes that have taken place in this country in the last decade. Since the housing bubble burst in 2008 producing the financial fallout that ushered in The Great Recession, it seems the middle class in this country has never really recovered, at least not uniformly.

Almost daily we hear about the one percent and the 99 percent. We hear about the great problem of income equality in this country. Millions of Americans it seems are making a lifestyle out of feeling disenfranchised and victimized by the wealthy class. People, especially young Americans, have been flocking to support presidential candidates simply on the basis of promised handouts; free college education, free healthcare, and the list goes on.

It saddens me that so many Americans today seem so willing to forfeit our most cherished freedoms guaranteed by our unique constitution in exchange for financial handouts from our increasingly paternal and egregiously meddling federal government. So many seem willing to accept government interference in every aspect of their lives, believing they need a financial crutch from the government just to make it through life. The saddest part about that is so many have apparently given up on the American dream, the belief that anyone in this country can prosper if he or she is willing to work hard and persevere.

To be sure, we have some problems in America that need to be addressed. But I've seen a lot of the world and have yet to find a place that offers the opportunities we have here. I've seen many places where people have no opportunities at all. Why do people from other countries flock here if it isn't because they expect to experience prosperity here that they could only dream of while living in the countries they were born in? This is still the land of opportunity.

It's my hope that at least some people who want a better life with greater financial security and flexibility will read this book and choose to learn and follow some principles that can help them achieve that rather than looking to the government to care for them from cradle to grave. Given how ineptly our financially illiterate professional class of elected politicians have managed to handle the finances of the federal government, you will forgive me if I choose to handle my finances on my own without depending on them.

Yes, I believe in the six strategies this book is about and am confident that used together they can empower people to build wealth. I could have simply created a website and posted all the information there. But how many would have read it, taken it seriously, or acted on it? The fact is, in this country we tend to equate value with cost. Perhaps you're familiar with this timeless quote, "What we obtain too cheap, we esteem too lightly." The meaning within that quote explains why I decided to write a book and offer it for sale rather than just giving the information away for free. If you buy this book with your own hard-earned money, even though the cover price is purposely set considerably below the cost of a latte from your favorite coffee purveyor, chances are you will read it and at least consider the information it contains.

2

First Secret: Start Building Wealth

One definition of wealth, as defined by Merriam-Webster is: "abundance of valuable material possessions or resources." We might say then that building wealth is the process of accumulating a large amount of money and stuff.

Certainly, you and I may define wealth quite differently. For some the term wealth conjures up mental images of palatial homes, luxury cars, private yachts, and vacations to exotic destinations. Others view wealth as simply having enough financial resources to live life comfortably and to have the ability to meet unexpected financial surprises without worrying they will be driven into bankruptcy. Being wealthy for some can be as simple as freedom from constant money worries.

That said, the principles behind the six secrets to building wealth are powerful. Acting on them will put you on the path to building real wealth and greater financial security. While you may never become a billionaire, you will become wealthy, perhaps wealthy beyond your wildest dreams.

Start building wealth by saving a part of your income

This first secret may seem so pedestrian and obvious that reading the heading for this section just now may have left you feeling a twinge of regret that you paid good money for this book. Allow me to remind you that I told you in the introduction to the book that these six secrets are nothing new. They are timeless common sense principles of personal money management that somehow have largely been forgotten. Don't simply dismiss out of hand the concept that saving a part of your income could possibly be a powerful wealth building principle. In fact, if you ever hope to build wealth, saving is a habit you must acquire.

To take the first step in building real wealth, you must not only save part of your income, you must establish the habit of saving ten percent of all that you earn. The ten percent principle is vitally important to your success. Saving one percent, three percent, or even nine percent will not suffice if you truly aspire to be wealthy. Frankly, I can't fully explain to you why saving ten percent is so important. I just know from personal experience that it is for reasons I don't pretend to completely understand. However, it's literally almost magical.

Simply saving ten percent of your income however is not the sum of the first secret to building wealth. You will have to do more. After all if that was all anyone had to do to become wealthy, everyone would be doing it. We would all be wealthy and there would be no need for books like this one.

It's important for me to note before going further, that saving ten percent of your income to satisfy this principle means that this ten percent is dedicated to one sole purpose. Any other savings you choose to do must be over and above this ten percent. There are many worthwhile things people save for and should. As examples we may save for retirement, something I'll be talking about more in a later chapter. Families may choose to save for their children's future college education expenses. It's good and responsible to save for all those kinds of things. But just remember, the ten percent required by this first principle has one singular purpose. Its sole purpose is to help you build wealth and it can't be used for other purposes, no matter how good and worthy those purposes are.

How then will the ten percent be used? You must invest the ten percent for long-term growth. When we get to the third secret to building wealth, we will look at specific ways to invest for long-term growth. For now, it's sufficient for you to simply know how the ten percent will be used.

Accomplishing this first secret by saving ten percent of your income and investing it for long-term growth is so powerful that if you do nothing else with what you learn from this book but that, if you don't bother learning or implementing a single one of the other six secrets, someday you will be wealthy and wealthier than you may even be able to imagine right now. When you establish the habit of saving ten percent of your income, year in and year out, it will radically improve your financial circumstances for the rest of your life. Following this principle alone will never allow you to become as wealthy as you might become if you learn and apply all six of the secrets, but will enable you to live the rest of your life comfortably without money worries.

Before leaving this first secret, there is one more thing you must understand. When it comes to saving ten percent of your income, you must pay yourself first. Pay yourself first is a phrase most of us have heard so many times that it has quite literally become a cliché. Just about any personal finance book you might ever read will mention paying yourself first. That's because it's good advice and necessary for a consistent savings program.

Paying yourself first means saving a portion of your income regularly, right off the top before you pay anything else. Cliché or not, paying yourself first is not only a great piece of advice, it is mandatory if you are truly serious about building wealth. You have to be ruthless and unwavering when it comes to paying yourself first. You must literally treat saving ten percent of your income from every paycheck like it is a bill that must be paid. I can practically guarantee you that if you do not develop the habit of paying yourself first, you will never escape living payday to payday and you will never acquire real wealth. It's that simple. Here is why.

Online lender CashNetUSA surveyed 1,000 people and found that 22% reported having less than $100 in savings to cover an emergency while 46% said they had less than $800 in savings. When asked why they weren't saving more the answer given by the overwhelming majority of respondents was that after paying for housing, car related expenses, childcare, debts, and other expenses there just wasn't enough money left over for saving more. The problem isn't that most of us don't know that we should be saving as a cushion against unexpected financial emergencies. The reason most people don't have adequate savings is because instead of paying themselves first, they pay all their other expenses first hoping there will be something left at the end for savings. Invariable there never is for those living paycheck to paycheck and the cycle just continues.

In the foreword to this book I noted that the definition of living paycheck to paycheck assumes having limited or no savings. The two go hand in hand. Think about your own situation for a moment. If faced with $1,000 bill for an unexpected emergency room visit or an unanticipated $500 car repair bill, do you have enough money in savings right now to cover them? If not, you're not alone. A survey by personal finance site Bankrate.com, found that 62 percent of Americans have no emergency savings to pay for unforeseen expenses like those.

The Bankrate.com survey results were supported by a similar survey conducted at about the same time by Google Consumer Survey for the personal finance website GOBankingRates.com. That survey found that approximately 62 percent of Americans have less than $1,000 in their savings accounts and 21 percent of Americans don't even have a savings account.

If you are determined to stop living paycheck to paycheck and serious about building wealth you must pay yourself first by designating ten percent of your earnings to savings every pay period. Your savings account deposit must come right off the top before you do anything else with your earnings.

Since I remember well saying it myself once, I easily can imagine you saying right now that you are barely making ends meet as it is and that there is absolutely no way that you can save ten percent of every paycheck or maybe even ten percent of any paycheck. My response to you however is this. Yes, you can. You can find a way.

Depending on your own circumstances, you may only have to make some adjustments to your budget and alter your spending habits to accommodate saving ten percent. On the other hand, if you don't make a lot and it takes nearly every penny of your paycheck just to keep food on the table, clothes on your back, and a roof over your head, you may think me very presumptuous to suggest that everyone should be able to save ten percent of his or her income. Without a doubt, it will be more difficult for some who read this book to do than for others.

We are all in different situations with respect to how much we earn and spend. I get that. So for those that have little fat in their spending habits to cut, a more creative approach and perhaps greater sacrifices will have to be made. It could mean taking on a part-time job, selling stuff, or finding some other means of adding other income streams. I don't minimize the difficulty it may present for some, but it can be done. To quote another cliché, "Where there is a will, there is a way." What you have to ask yourself is whether you are willing to make short-term sacrifices now to escape living paycheck to paycheck and building wealth for the rest of your life.

Once you accept the idea of saving ten percent of your income for your greater long-term good, and make the decision to do it, don't rely on willpower. Those who are or have formerly been members in good standing of the living payday to payday club are not known for our willpower or self-discipline when it comes to money management. Put your decision on automatic and then you don't have to think about it. Set it and forget it.

First open a savings account, if you don't have one already have one. Then set up automatic transfers of the ten percent of your earnings to your savings account. I'm able to do that through my employer by payroll deduction. That's a great way to do it. But if your employer doesn't offer that option, you can set it up with your bank to transfer the ten percent from your checking account to your savings account on the dates that coincide with the frequency of your paychecks. For example, if you are paid bi-weekly set up bi-weekly transfers.

Finally, don't forget to save ten percent of any irregular income like occasional bonuses from work or tax refunds. The goal here is to save the first ten percent of every dollar of income that comes into your possession.

If you've never forced yourself to save, especially by putting it on automatic so you aren't tempted to skip doing it, it really won't be as painful an experience as you may imagine. I promise you that you will very quickly adjust to living on the remaining ninety percent of your income. In fact quite quickly you won't even miss the ten percent going into savings.

Don't allow the amount of your paychecks to discourage you from starting and developing the habit of saving the first ten percent of your earnings. Whether you earn an annual six figure income or hold a minimum wage job, saving that ten percent month after month, year after year is going to result in a significant and positive change in your financial circumstances. And when you get those periodic pay raises, don't neglect to increase the amount of your automatic transfers to savings.

Get your most recent paycheck stub or pay slip. Find the amount under net pay. Using a calculator or pen and paper multiply that amount by .10. The result represents ten percent of your income, the amount you should start saving beginning with your very next paycheck and should continue saving every pay period thereafter.

If you don't already have a savings account, before your very next payday, visit your bank or other financial institution of your choice. Find out how much is required to open a basic savings account. The minimum opening deposit at my bank is only $25. Many financial institutions, especially credit unions, require only $5 to open a basic savings account. Then before continuing to the next chapter, find the money for the required initial deposit and open a savings account.

Once you have calculated your ten percent savings figure, made that first deposit to a savings account, and have set up your automatic transfer, you will have taken the first step towards building wealth.

More importantly you will have taken a big step towards escaping forever the living paycheck to paycheck cycle.

Before leaving the subject of saving, let me reiterate something. If you don't earn a lot don't convince yourself ten percent of each paycheck wouldn't amount to enough to make any real difference. With time and compound interest, even a modest monthly amount deposited to savings would make a big difference. Even if you save only $30 a month to start, as your income rises, the ten percent savings will rise too. Thirty dollars will become $40, then a $100, and then hundreds of dollars per month. Your savings will grow to a significant amount faster than you may even imagine.

3

Second Secret: Spend Less Than You Earn

As powerful as saving and investing ten percent of your income for long-term growth is, if you truly aspire to build real wealth you must also develop the habit of spending less than you earn. Spending less than you earn is the way you create discretionary income to save.

Spending less than you earn

To spend less than you earn you need a tool. That tool is a detailed written budget. Having a budget is fundamental to spending less than you earn. I believe that it is impossible to build real wealth without having and following a budget.

A 2014 study by the National Foundation for Credit Counseling found that 60 percent of Americans admit to not having a personal finance budget. That percentage seems eerily similar to the estimated percentage of Americans that various financial studies have shown are living paycheck to paycheck. I don't think that's a coincidence. Those living paycheck to paycheck are very likely the same individuals and families that don't have or don't follow a household budget.

Without a detailed written budget, there is no realistic way to know where your money is going or whether you are spending too much in particular areas. It's just not possible to keep a budget in your head and maintain adequate control over your spending. Unfortunately that is exactly what too many people try to do. Predictably many of those are the people that end up living paycheck to paycheck. I know because I've been there. I was once one of those people. I lived paycheck to paycheck. It wasn't until I found myself grappling with a serious financial crisis that I finally learned how necessary a budget really is.

Budget formats

Some people, especially those who have never had one, find the very idea of creating a budget a bit intimidating. There is no need to feel intimidated. It isn't difficult to make a budget, even for the first time.

There are many formats that can be used for making a budget. I prefer to create my monthly budgets as Excel spreadsheets. This allows me to insert formulas that automatically total the major categories. At a glance I can easily see how the totals of each major category change month to month. That can quickly alert me if I'm starting to get off track by overspending in some of the categories.

One of the best things about using a spreadsheet is that I can copy and paste the budget from the previous month to quickly make my budget for the current month. All I have to do then is make minor adjustments. It is a real time saver not having to start from scratch each time.

If you want to use a spreadsheet but don't have Excel and don't want to spend the money to buy Microsoft Office, there is a free open source office suite called Open Office that has a spreadsheet program that is very similar to Excel.

Perhaps spreadsheets are not your thing but you would still like to create and keep your budget using your computer. If so, EveryDollar (www.everydollar.com) might be the ticket. EveryDollar is free budget software accessible from your computer or iPhone.

Another simple option that can be used is a spiral bound household budget book with pre-printed budget categories and line items that are available from office supply stores and other retailers for around $5. Lastly, you can always use the simplest budgeting method of all, the old-school pen and paper method. That is what I used for several years when I first started making budgets. It is every bit as effective as the most modern computerized options. The real point is to make and follow a budget. The format you choose to use is simply a matter of personal preference.

Creating a budget step by step

For those who have never created a monthly budget, it really isn't difficult to do once you understand the layout, what should be included, and how to categorize the expenses portion. Here is how to layout a simple household budget, step by step.

1. At the top of your budget list your income from your primary job, income from any part-time job if applicable, and any other sources of regular income you receive on at least a monthly basis.

2. In keeping with "pay yourself first" tenet advocated by the six secrets to building wealth system, list savings directly beneath income. Multiply the total income figure calculated during the first step above by .10 to calculate the monthly figure for budgeted savings.

3. Next list your fixed expenses. Fixed expenses are those you pay every month that are always the same amount. Examples include expenses like:

- Mortgage or rent.
- Car loan payment(s).
- Personal loan payments (including student loans) with a fixed payment.
- Auto insurance premiums.
- Life insurance premiums.
- Health insurance premiums (if not paid by payroll deduction).
- Telephone bill.
- Cable television bill.

The above is not an exhaustive list. Just list under fixed expenses every expense you pay every month that is always the same amount.

Because fixed expenses are typically owed under some sort of contractual agreement that requires you to pay a fixed amount each month, this is the expense category where you have little or no control with respect to choosing to reduce the amounts paid each month.

4. Next list your variable expenses. Variable expenses are simply those expenses you pay monthly but that vary in amount from month to month. Examples include:

- Utility bills (electric, gas, water, sanitation).
- Groceries.
- Credit card payments.
- Out of pocket medical expenses (prescriptions, co-pays, etc.).

Again the above is not an exhaustive list but should help you understand what expenses to list under the variable category. Variable expenses are expenses that you do have some control over with respect to how much you spend. As an example, you can choose how much to spend on groceries each month. You can also in theory reduce the amount of your electric bill or water bill by using less. While at least the minimum must be paid on credit cards to remain current, you can of course always pay more than the minimum if you wish and can afford to. Also, if you stop using your credit cards your balance will be reduced with each payment even if you only pay the minimum. As your balance decreases, so will the amount of your required minimum payment. This will in turn reduce your total credit card expenses each month.

5. The last category is discretionary expenses. These are all the other things you spend money on each month. The total amount you have to spend on discretionary expenses is the total amount of your income left after you subtract savings, fixed expenses, and variable expenses. Some examples of discretionary expenses are:

- Entertainment and recreation.

- Dining out.
- Clothing allowance.
- Other miscellaneous expenses.

Discretionary expenses is the category over which you have the most control in determining how much you spend. If you need to cut expenses, these expenses are the ones you generally would look at reducing first.

Now that you have learned how to create a budget, let's look at some budget guidelines.

Budget guidelines

Certain expenses which we might term "budget wreckers" are those that many people often have trouble controlling and overspend on. They represent one of the primary causes behind people ending up living paycheck to paycheck. Many of them are areas I struggled with during the years I lived paycheck to paycheck.

Something I found helpful back then was the discovery of some budget guidelines on what percentage of a person's total monthly income should be consumed by certain budget categories. It was a real eye opener for me. I discovered these recommended percentages reading a personal finance book written by the late Larry Burkett, an author and radio personality whose life work focused on financial counseling. Here are some of his guidelines which I believe are both reasonable and relevant for most people.

The percentages shown for each expense category represents the maximum percent of your monthly income that should be spent on the respective expense category.

- Housing expense - 36% (Includes mortgage/rent payment, insurance, property taxes, repairs and maintenance).
- Auto expense - 12% (Include car loan payments, insurance, tags and taxes, gasoline, repairs and maintenance).

- Food - 12% (Groceries and meals out).
- Life insurance - 5%
- Entertainment and Recreation - 6%
- Clothing expense - 5%
- Medical and dental expenses - 4% (Out of pocket).
- Debt - 5% (Personal loans and credit card payments).
- Savings - 10%
- Miscellaneous expenses - 5%

The above percentages can be used as guidelines for establishing budgeting goals. If you are creating a budget for the first time, don't be surprised if your current spending levels exceed many if not all of the above recommended percentages. Mine certainly did when I first started making and following a budget. In particular I was overspending on housing, auto expenses, and by a wide margin debt.

At least when you are just starting the practice of keeping a budget, it isn't a real problem if you spend more than the recommended percentages on specific expense categories as long as the sum of your actual percentages doesn't exceed 100 percent. If it does that is a problem because it indicates you are living beyond your means and need to reduce your monthly expenses, find a way to generate additional income, or a combination of the two. Over time, you should work towards reducing your expenses in categories that are significantly higher than the recommended budget category percentages to improve your financial circumstances.

Debt

If the percentage of your income consumed by debt payments is significantly higher than the recommended five percent, it indicates that you are carrying too much debt and are too reliant on credit to make ends meet. It also indicates you need to create a plan to lower your debt, the sooner the better.

According to the Nerd Wallet website, the average U.S. household in 2015 had $15,355 in credit card debt. Further the site reports that the average household is paying $6,658 in credit card interest per year. That is truly an indefensible waste of financial resources in most cases. Carrying balances and making minimum monthly payments on credit cards is another sure fire way to keep yourself trapped living paycheck to paycheck. Consider just one example.

A hypothetical person has a credit card that carries an interest rate of 23 percent. His current balance owed is $2,500.00. If he chooses to make only the minimum monthly payments until the balance is paid off, assuming he doesn't charge another dime on the card, it will take him about 15 years to pay off the balance. Over that 15 years he will pay interest charges of around $6,350.00. According to a recent Gallup survey, the average number of cards owned among Americans with credit cards is 3.7. Imagine now that our hypothetical consumer has two or three other credit cards with similar interest rates that he also carries balances on and pays only the minimum monthly payments. You should easily be able to imagine just how much of his income over the next 15 years is going to be eaten up by interest charges.

I'm not against credit cards. I have several of them in my wallet right now and occasionally use them. Credit cards can be a useful financial tool. It's much safer to use a credit card for online purchases than it is to use a debit card. There are also advantages to using a credit card over a debit card for things like renting a car or confirming a hotel reservation. But making purchases on a credit card, carrying a balance month to month, and paying only minimum payments rather than paying them in full at the end of every month is simply poor money management. I know because I've been there. There was a time when I used credit cards to buy things I couldn't afford and then paid for those things with interest for years afterwards.

Debt for most people is not only the biggest budget wrecker, debt is also a wealth killer. I'm not saying all debt is bad. It's not. But if you expect to get off the paycheck to paycheck train and build wealth you have to minimize debt. Reserve debt for major purchases like buying a home or a car. Develop the habit of buying other things only when you have saved enough to pay for them in full.

There are a number of things that people aren't aware of or at least don't think about when it comes to using credit. One thing too many people don't know is that using more than about 30 percent of your total available credit really hurts your credit score. The further you go above 30 percent the more harm you do to your perceived credit worthiness. Having a low credit score costs you in many insidious ways. A low credit score means that even when you are extended credit, you pay a much higher interest rate than someone with a higher credit score. You also will likely pay more for your auto insurance with a low credit score. Most auto insurance companies today take your credit score into consideration when rating your policy and computing your premium. Insurers justify that by claiming that research shows there is a direct correlation between a person's credit score and the risk of that person being in claims producing accidents.

The main take away from this portion of our discussion is that credit card debt is always bad debt when you carry balances on your credit cards. This habit will invariably keep you broke and living paycheck to paycheck. Real wealth will always elude you. I know from bitter experience that is undeniably true. One of the keys to building wealth is to payoff credit card debt as quickly as possible and resolve to never carry credit card balances again.

Adopt a strategy to pay off your debt

The first step in getting out of debt is to stop using it. One suggestion by some credit counselors is to put your credit cards into a water filled container and to then place the container in your freezer which of course results in your credit cards being encased in a solid block of ice. This at least theoretically means that you won't go to the trouble of thawing out the cards to use them for impulse purchases. In other words you won't be as tempted to use credit cards as you would if you simply continue to carry them in your wallet or handbag.

When I made the decision to stop using plastic for things I couldn't afford, I simply removed the cards from my wallet and put them in a drawer. That served to dissuade me from using them for impulse purchases and forced me to think seriously about whether a considered purchase on credit was really a necessity. That worked for me. Just pick the strategy that works for you. If just putting them away in a drawer is an effective deterrent then there is no need to result to the block of ice method. But if the strategy you choose doesn't work and you continue to use credit to buy things you really can't afford, you may very well have to resort to the nuclear option and cut them up.

Once you stop the hemorrhaging cash by not continuing to run up more debt, the next step is to adopt a plan to pay off your debt. There are two primary schools of thought when it comes to the most effective way of paying of debt. Both involve a "snowball" effect in the sense that money formerly used to make monthly payments on one debt after it has been paid off is added to the monthly payment of the next debt targeted for pay off so that it gets paid off faster.

With either option, you concentrate on paying off one debt at a time, paying as much as you possibly can on a single debt while making minimum monthly payments on the rest. As more debts are paid off, the amount of money you have available to pay on the next debt targeted for payoff grows or "snowballs" so the longer you stick with the program the faster you get out of debt. Now let's look at the two options.

The first option is to list all your debts by the balance owed, from smallest to largest. You start by paying off those with the smallest balances. Proponents of this method believe that since you will see faster results by paying off several small debts relatively quickly, you will stay motivated to get rid of debt since you will gain momentum quickly.

The second method is to list all your debts by the interest rate you pay, from highest to lowest rates. Then you start by paying off those with the highest interest rates without regard to the balances owed. This method makes the most sense from a purely financial standpoint because over the long-term you are going to save more on interest charges. But as some financial experts point out, since you will see results much slower following this plan, chances are much greater that you will lose motivation and fail to follow through on your decision to get out of debt as soon as possible.

I see the merit in both methods. I experimented with both methods when I decided it was time to get out of debt. The second method is undeniably the most cost effective. By paying down and eventually paying off the debts with the highest interest rates first, you do easily save the most money. But in my case, the credit cards that carried the highest interest rates also represented the ones I had the highest balances on and took the longest time to pay off. I opted for the first method and attacked the debts with the smallest balances first. I saw almost immediate results on my monthly cash outflows and that motivated me to stick with my debt playoff plan.

While you should choose the method that makes the most sense to you, in my case it was worth it to pay more interest in the long run to build my debt snowball faster. For one thing I really didn't have any extra money to put towards my debts. The snowball effect was the only realistic option for getting more money to apply towards my larger debts. And I benefitted psychologically because seeing the accounts with the smaller balances being paid off relatively quickly gave me a little instant gratification that went a long ways toward sustaining my momentum and motivation to become debt free as soon as possible.

While I've focused primarily on credit card debt in this section, when you decide to implement a debt payoff strategy do of course list all your debts other than your mortgage if you have one. I am in favor of accelerating mortgage payoffs too to become completely debt free but for a number of good financial reasons, that should always be the very last debt you payoff.

To summarize the principles of this chapter and the second secret to building wealth, next to saving ten percent of your income, spending less than you earn by taking control of your spending is the the second most important step you can take to stop living paycheck to paycheck and start building wealth. Taking control of your spending also means getting out of debt and staying out.

Before moving on to the next chapter, choose a format and create a budget. Just learning and understanding the six secrets is not enough. You have to put them into practice. Once you have made a budget, look for the problem spending areas that you need to focus on reducing first. Start thinking about whether you just need to tighten your belt a little to stick with an effective budget or whether you need to start thinking of doing something to increase your income. Learning is good, but it is always acting on what you learn that is actually going to make a real difference.

4

Third Secret: Grow Your Wealth

In this chapter you're going to learn two very important things. We have finally reached the point where I'm going to talk about exactly how to use the ten percent savings principle to escape living paycheck to paycheck and start building wealth. In addition, after reading this chapter I'm confident you will start to see how all six of the secrets work together to build a complete, comprehensive, and powerful wealth building personal financial plan.

Hopefully by this point you have not only read and acquired some basic knowledge about personal finance, but have taken some concrete steps towards applying what you have learned. You should have opened a savings account if you didn't have one before starting this book. You should have created a monthly budget. Finally, you should have at the very least started thinking about what plan you will use to get out of debt. I hope you have taken those important steps because that is exactly what will help you get the most from the information in this book.

Prioritizing the use of your ten percent savings

As important as saving ten percent of your income is in taking full advantage of the six wealth building secrets this book is about, there are some important priorities that have to be established and followed to leverage those savings to build wealth.

By priorities I mean using your savings to accomplish one purpose before using the money for another purpose. There is definitely a hierarchy to it. Don't try to do two things at once. Instead focus on your first priority until you have accomplished its underlying financial goal. Then and only then, shift your focus to the next priority on the list.

I'm going to share with you the priority list I used to get away from living paycheck to paycheck and to start building wealth. It is what worked for me. After looking at my list of priorities you may feel you want to arrange your priorities differently. But I will only recommend something that I know from personal experience works. If you decide to arrange your priorities differently from what I suggest, your results may be different.

Establish an emergency fund

The first priority in my opinion for the use of your ten percent savings is the establishment of an emergency fund. An emergency fund is in a sense a financial life preserver that will save you if you're hit by a large, unexpected financial expense that must be paid. Let me offer a few examples; a large unexpected auto repair bill, an expensive medical or dental emergency, the cost of repairing or replacing a major appliance that suddenly stops working. Without an emergency fund to pay for unexpected financial surprises like those, by necessity you must turn to credit to fill the gap. That is one of the major reasons people get sucked into the living paycheck to paycheck trap to begin with.

The best place to keep your emergency fund savings is in a basic savings account because it allows you to get at the money when you need it. Because the types of expenses an emergency fund is intended to deal with are unexpected, you generally need the money to pay for them now, not in a week or perhaps even a few days.

Many personal finance experts recommend that you establish an emergency fund with a balance that equals 3-6 months of your income. I can see the wisdom of that under certain circumstances but I believe that a $1,000.00 emergency fund is adequate for most people trying to escape living paycheck to paycheck. That's usually enough to pay for most of the unexpected expenses that people who don't have an emergency fund end up putting on credit cards. I also think that after establishing a $1,000.00 emergency fund, there are lots of better options for your savings than to park your money in a low interest bearing savings account.

At the time I was writing this book, according to the financial information website Bankrate, the highest savings rates being paid was one percent. One percent may be better than nothing, but not by much.

Once you have achieved a $1,000.00 savings account balance to serve as an emergency fund, it's time to start looking at more profitable ways to invest your ten percent savings.

Payoff debt

Debt and paying off debt was discussed in the previous chapter. But here we are going to look at paying off a debt from a different perspective. Perhaps you have never thought of it this way, but paying off debt can be viewed as an investment. In fact it may very well be the best and most profitable investment you will ever make and here is why.

Let's look at credit cards for a moment. The current average interest rates charged on credit cards are between 15-28 percent. Those living paycheck to paycheck typically have the lowest credit scores and so generally have cards that charge the highest rates. It is very difficult to find an investment that consistently returns anything near 15-28 percent. Using the stock market as an example, since 1925, using the S&P 500 as the benchmark, stocks have a historical compounded annual return of 11.2 percent. That's not bad but it is significantly less than the interest rates most people pay on credit card balances. Yes, paying off high interest debt isn't going to immediately put any money in your bank account but over the long run, getting rid of debt is going to pay off big when it comes to building wealth.

Paying off high interest debt, unlike most other high yield investments, is completely risk free. It's an investment that consistently returns guaranteed rates of 15-28 percent. Those returns by the way are absolutely tax free. It's truly a no-brainer. Once you have stablished your emergency fund, if you have high interest debt, don't even think about investing your ten percent savings anywhere else until you have paid off your high interest debt.

Investing

If you are one of the fortunate Americans without high interest debt or once you have paid off all your high interest debt, it's time to move forward to the third priority, investing your ten percent savings in something that actually does increase your income and puts money in your bank account.

There is a dizzying array of investment options available to choose from. Mutual funds, exchange traded funds, individual stocks and bonds, certificates of deposit, money market accounts, commodities futures, precious metals, and real estate, just to name a very few.

Some of the options for investing, we can discount right away when our goal is to stop living paycheck to paycheck and start building wealth. Real estate for example for the most part requires significant sums of money just to get started. It also often requires the use of debt for leverage. Real estate is arguably one of the best wealth building investments available. Although it might be an option in the future, it just isn't the place for most people to get started building wealth.

While I could spend time and multiple pages here explaining all the different investing options along with their advantages and disadvantages, I'm not going to do that. Instead I'm going to tell you what I believe is very best place for investing your ten percent savings. While my opinion on where you can most profitably invest your savings is based on my own personal experiences, it is also backed up by decades of solid data.

Understand that investing is a long-term pursuit. When you are considering your investment options don't look at what a potential investment has done over the past few months, the past year, or even the last three years. Instead look at the historical long-term performance of any investment you are considering. While past performance is no guarantee of future results, the long-term track record of a particular investment type is a valid metric to use when deciding what type of investment is most likely to give you the best returns over the long run.

Let's look at the historical performances of some of the options you could choose from to invest your savings in. Over the past 20 years, US Treasury bills have returned an average of 4%. Corporate bonds have returned an average of 6%. The average actively managed mutual fund has returned an average 8%. Stocks (using the S&P 500 as the benchmark) have returned an average of 11 %. Interestingly, the 40 year and 60 year average returns of each of those four investment classes are the same. What that illustrates is that stocks have consistently earned more than any other investment class over the long term, despite the regular ups and downs in the market. Here is another illustration of that.

According to Ibbotson Associates, a financial research and information company, $100 invested in short-term investments (like certificates of deposit or short-term treasuries) in 1926 would have grown to $2,100 by 2015. That same $100 invested in corporate bonds in 1926 would have increased to $9,800 by 2015. Had that hypothetical $100 been invested in stocks in 1926, by 2015 the investment would have risen to $544,200! As you should see, just a few percentage points over the long haul make a tremendous difference in total return on investment.

While stocks are but one of many possible ways to invest your ten percent savings, when your objective is to build wealth there just isn't any reason to invest in any other asset class. Over the long-term stocks provide the the highest potential returns of any type of investment hands down.

Now that I've laid out what I hope is a convincing case for investing in stocks, let's look at some of the different ways you can invest in stocks. Here I am going to take time and space to discuss some options because there is more than one way to invest in stocks. We will also look at some of the advantages and disadvantages of each of those options.

Mutual funds

Americans invested $102 billion in mutual funds in 2014 alone. By year-end 2014, mutual funds had nearly $16 trillion in assets under management. Those figures illustrate the popularity of mutual funds as a way to invest in the stock market. The popularity of mutual funds as an investment choice isn't surprising since mutual fund investing does offer some advantages.

There are many different types of mutual funds, but for the sake of simplicity we will look at only the four major flavors. Funds that invest primarily in stocks are called equity funds. Funds that principally invest in income securities like government and corporate bonds are called fixed income funds. Those that invest mostly in short-term fixed income securities are known as money market funds. The fourth category, balanced funds invest in a mix of stocks and fixed income securities. Since stocks offer the highest potential returns of any asset class, the remainder of this section will focus on equity funds, those which invest primarily in stocks.

Most funds are actively managed by a financial and investing professional. The fund manager makes the investment decisions about what specific securities the fund buys and sells. You could say then that mutual funds represent a passive approach to investing in the stock market. For many investors, that is one of the attractions for investing in mutual funds. Those who don't have the time or inclination to do the necessary research required to choose individual stocks can simply buy shares in a mutual fund and leave the stock picking to a professional.

One way to think of a mutual fund is a pool of money contributed by thousands of individual investors. The fund manager then takes the money and invests it in hundreds of different stocks. That by the way is another major attraction for those who invest in mutual funds, instant diversification.

Diversification is a means of reducing risk by allocating your investments among the stocks of many different companies in different industries and other categories. Instead of putting all your eggs in one basket by investing all your money in one stock, you invest in many stocks with the goal of maximizing your return by owning stocks in different industries and sectors that would all react differently to the same event. While diversification does not guarantee against loss, it is the most important component of minimizing the risk of loss when it comes to investing in stocks. Few of us have anywhere near enough money to invest to achieve diversification on the scale that a mutual fund does.

Each share owned in a fund represents a minute fractional share in every share of stock the fund owns. This means that each individual investor shares in the fortunes of the fund. When the stock portfolio of the fund appreciates in value, the values of the shares held in the mutual fund appreciate proportionally. When a fund sells shares of stock it owns at a profit or receives dividends, the fund distributes a portion of the capital gains or dividends to each investor based on the number of shares held in the fund. Since both capital gains and dividends distributed by mutual funds are typically reinvested, you only get money in your pocket when you sell shares in a mutual fund for more than you paid for them.

One last advantage to investing in stocks by putting your money into a mutual fund is you can buy shares directly from the mutual fund and so do not have to pay commissions to a stock broker to buy and sell mutual fund shares as you would have to do when buying individual shares of stock on your own. However, mutual funds are not a free ride. Mutual fund owners pay fees to the fund to pay the fund manager and to defray the costs of operating the fund.

According to Morningstar, an investment research and investment management firm, the average fee ratio charged by actively managed funds is 1.25%. That may not sound like much but since actively managed funds historically have returned an average of 8%, taking 1.25% off the top reduces that historical average to 6.75%. That then is the first disadvantage to mutual fund investing.

The preceding brings up another disadvantage to investing through mutual funds. Since stocks historical average a return of 11% over any 20 year period you look at, the fact that the average mutual fund returns 8% over those same periods (6.75% after accounting for fees), it's obvious that most actively managed mutual funds underperform the S&P 500, the benchmark used to evaluate how well or poorly a fund does.

Actually most mutual funds, 80% in fact according to Morningstar, underperform the broader stock market year after year. While there are some valid reasons that happens that aren't necessarily attributable to poor fund management, that in my opinion is reason enough to avoid putting your hard-earned dollars into actively managed mutual funds. Why invest in something that more often than not doesn't perform at least as well as the broader stock market? Especially when there exists another investing option that virtually guarantees you can obtain returns that very closely mimic the annual returns of the S&P 500 broad market index. There is no reason to settle for something in the neighborhood of a 6.75% return after fees when you can get something close to 11%. And that provides the perfect place for us to move this discussion along to the second method of investing in stocks, exchange traded funds or ETFs.

Exchange traded funds

Although the first American ETF wasn't launched until 1993, over the intervening years exchange-traded funds have become one of the most popular investment vehicles for both institutional and individual investors. ETFs now have over $1 trillion in assets under management.

Exchange traded funds operate very much like mutual funds but are promoted as cheaper (lower fees) and superior alternatives to mutual funds. Like mutual funds ETFs offer instant diversification in that buying a share in an exchange traded fund gives you a minute stake in the basket of hundreds of stocks the ETF is invested in. Unlike mutual funds, where share price is only calculated at the end of each stock market trading day, ETFs trade on the stock exchange just like individual stocks. The price of an ETF share can change virtually each time shares are bought and sold.

ETFs offer convenient and affordable exposure to a huge range of markets and investment categories. There are actively managed ETFs just like their mutual fund counterparts. But a major attraction to ETF investing for many investors is the concept of index investing. For example you can buy shares in a number of exchange traded funds that are designed to replicate as closely as possible the annual return of broad market indexes like the S&P 500 index. Those ETFs are quite successful at doing that. The actual returns from indexed ETFs vary only slightly from the underlying indexes and that difference is simply attributable to the fees charged investors by the funds.

To be fair, mutual funds also offer index funds but invariably charge investors higher fees than exchange traded funds do. While ETFs do charge fees like mutual funds do, the fees are considerable lower which is what makes ETFs lower cost. Many funds are available to investors today with a 0.20 percent expense ratio ($20 annually per $10,000 invested) or less. Compare that to the average 1.25% expense ratio charged by actively mutual funds.

Since ETFs trade on the stock market just like individual stocks, potentially at least you must pay brokerage commissions when buying and selling shares of an exchange traded fund. Even discount brokers commissions that range from $4.95 to $9.99 per trade can really add up and eat into your returns over time. However, most discount brokers offer a list of ETFs that they allow investors to trade commission fee. By selecting a broker that has the specific ETF you're interested in on its trade for free list, you avoid paying costly commissions.

The bottom line is that ETFs offer most of the advantages of a mutual fund including instant diversification, but at lower fees. For investors who opt for a hands off, passive stock investing strategy rather over buying individual stocks and managing their own portfolios, investing in indexed ETFs can be the smarter and more cost effective way to go in comparison to owning mutual funds.

In my opinion, the only real disadvantage to investing your savings in indexed exchange traded funds is that you are limited to just matching the returns of the broader market index that such ETFs attempt to replicate.

While ETFs haven't been around as long as mutual funds, in practice they work in much the same way. That makes it a safe bet that over 10, 20, or 30 years, the average returns from exchange traded funds are going to be about the same as the historical long-term average returns of mutual funds, which as you may recall is about 8%. There remains one more stock investing option to consider that can potentially return a lot more over the long run.

Individual stocks

More than 15 years ago, I was confronted by the fact that my finances were a shambles. I simply couldn't continue to live in denial and came to the realizations that my approach to managing money had to change and change radically. I made the commitment to do that. I started reading personal finance books and slowly but surely began educating myself and acquiring basic personal finance skills. One by one I started discovering and implementing these same six secrets to wealth that I'm sharing in this book.

I started paying myself first by saving ten percent of my income. I made and followed my first budgets. After less than five months I managed to establish a $1,000 emergency fund. I then focused on digging myself out of debt, which in my case took nearly three years. Once I had established the habit of saving and had paid off my high interest debt life was good and the money worries that often kept me up at night all but disappeared. But I wasn't satisfied. I not only wanted to escape living paycheck to paycheck, I wanted to build a secure financial future. I wanted to build wealth.

Through those years I was paying off debt, I kept searching, kept studying, and just as importantly kept saving. I started to learn about investing, the alternative to simply depositing my savings in a low interest savings account every payday that offered the potential of much higher returns. When I first had money to invest, I still didn't know enough about investing to know exactly where the best place to invest was. So like many people, I initially took the path of least resistance and invested my savings in mutual funds.

That wasn't a terrible decision. I did make some money investing in mutual funds and did start building wealth. I certainly did better than I would have had I just kept my money parked in a basic savings account or used it to buy CDs. But in time I started learning about buying individual stocks and how owning stocks could potentially beat the returns I was getting at the time from my mutual fund investments by a substantial margin. I then started to focus my investing self-education on the ins and outs of buying stocks.

It didn't happen overnight. I didn't just decide one day to dump all my mutual funds and dive into buying individual stocks. But gradually, as my confidence in what I was learning grew, I started transitioning away from mutual fund investing to investing in individual stocks. Once that transition was complete, I've never looked back.

I soon discovered that owning individual stocks was the very best approach to building wealth. Consider these facts.

With only very few exceptions like the onset of the Great Depression in 1929, the Dot -com bubble collapse from 1997-2000, and the Great Recession encompassing roughly 2007-2009, during the 20th century, stocks have returned an average of 11 percent per year.

Yes, in some years stocks returned much less than 11 percent and in others much more, but still a hypothetical investor who invested just $1,000 in an index fund in 1900 (had index funds existed then) would have had an investment worth $19.8 million by the end of 1999, assuming he or she had lived to the ripe old age of 99. If you invested $15,000 in stocks and managed to earn a 15 percent return on your investment, it would take only 30 years to turn your $15,000 into a cool $1 million.

But isn't choosing good stocks to buy hard, and aren't stocks risky? Besides, you might be thinking, I don't know squat about investing in stocks. That may all be true my friend, but no one knew anything about investing in stocks until he or she started to learn about it. It's hard to imagine, but there was in fact a day when the great Warren Buffett, widely recognized as the most successful investor of all time, didn't know squat about picking stocks. But obviously, he made the time and put forth the effort to educate himself on his way to becoming the most successful investor of all time. I did too. No, I'm not in the class of a Warren Buffett, but over time I've learned how to competently choose stocks that make me money and that help me build wealth. And you can too. All you have to do is leverage the time it takes for you to build your emergency fund and to pay off your high interest debt by studying and learning how to invest in stocks. There are countless numbers of excellent books available on the subject.

There is of course risk involved in investing in individual stocks. As any investment professional worth his salt will always tell you, past performance is no guarantee of future results. Stock markets are volatile and stocks can decline, sometimes significantly in response to adverse issuer, political, regulatory, market, or economic developments. You can lose money buying stocks.

Many a high flying stock of companies once the darlings of Wall Street have fallen on hard times and their stock prices have subsequently come crashing to earth. Companies can go bankrupt and the value of their stocks can literally fall to zero. Ever heard of the Enron Corporation for example? But many US companies have been in business and have earned profits for 100 years and more. During that time they have rewarded their shareholders with substantial returns. It isn't so much that buying and owning stocks is risky, it's more buying and owning bad stocks of poorly run companies is risky. Educating yourself on how to effectively evaluate stocks can enable you to avoid bad stocks for the most part and pick good ones. Everyone, and I mean everyone occasionally picks a stock that turns into a loser. The trick is to cut your losses in those situations quickly and to manage to pick good stocks more often than you pick bad ones.

Individual stocks are a riskier investment than mutual funds or ETFs, but along with the greater risks comes the potential for greater rewards. That's just how our free market system works. Risk little, earn little. Risk more, earn more. I never recommend blatant speculation, something like investing in penny stocks for example, but taking the calculated risks associated with buying the stocks of some of America's most successful companies can potentially reward you with exceptional returns on your investment.

Previously in the discussions on mutual funds and ETFs I spoke of diversification and why that's so important to investors. Most of us will never have the money to diversify our own portfolios on the scale of a fund that has millions or tens of millions to invest. But you can obtain reasonable diversification with your own portfolio of individual stocks. You have to diversify to spread your risk.

You diversify by not investing all your money in one stock. A good rule of thumb for a personal portfolio is to own five or six different stocks. Owning fewer stocks than that and you won't be diversified. Owning more and you probably won't spend enough time to stay on top of them by doing the requisite amount of homework. Don't concentrate all of your holding in one industry, or one sector. Instead aim for holding stocks in different industries and sectors.

When you are just starting out, you likely won't be able to diversify immediately by buying multiple stocks all at once. You may very well have to acquire them one at a time. That's okay, just don't forget about diversification. Once you have built a stake in one stock, start looking for a good stock in another industry or sector and start building a position in that one. Continue that strategy until you have achieved reasonable diversification.

Picking stocks isn't rocket science. Anyone with an interest in learning how to do it and who possesses the mathematical skills most of us had learned by fifth grade, can become a competent investor. But of course reading this short section on investing in individual stocks isn't going to do that. You've only been introduced to the idea and the possibilities of investing in stocks. You've only scratched the surface. If investing in individual stocks is a strategy of wealth building that interests you, get some of the good books on stock investing that are out there and start educating yourself. One of my favorites that I highly recommend to beginners is *The Motley Fool Investment Guide* by David and Tom Gardner. It's a complete primer on getting started with investing in individual stocks. The book won't make you an expert but after reading it, you will be knowledgeable enough to sensibly think about buying your first stock.

We've covered a lot of ground in this chapter, so let's summarize the most important takeaways from the third secret, growing your wealth.

- Remember the priorities. Don't start investing until you have established a $1,000 emergency fund and have paid off all of your high interest debt.

- Leverage the time spent saving your emergency fund and paying off debt by reading and educating yourself on the stock market and learning how to invest. You have plenty of time to study the stock market and learn how to wisely choose stocks to invest in, long before you ever place your first order with a broker.

- Choose the investment strategy that suits you personally. While I believe buying and owning individual stocks is the best way to build wealth, should you decide that mutual funds or ETFs are better suited to your temperament and level of risk tolerance that's fine. Just understand your returns will be less but that can be a small price to pay for peace of mind.

- Don't invest money in the stock market that you are unable or unwilling to leave there for at least three years, preferably longer. Time is a critical component of building wealth through investing.

- Don't invest in individual stocks until you have taken the time to educate yourself on how to sensibly pick stocks.

- Never, I say again, never invest in anything you don't fully understand.

- Make your own investment decisions. Don't ever buy an investment based on a tip from a co-worker, a friend, a talking head on one of the business channels, or your brother-in-law. Tips like that may be a legitimate way to learn about potential investments but should only be the starting point for doing your own research.

- Always be able to articulate the reasons why you are investing in a particular stock and what you expect to gain by buying that stock.

Now, without further ado, let's spring forward into the next chapter where you will learn about the fourth secret.

5

Fourth Secret: Protect Your Wealth from Loss

Protecting your wealth against loss covers a good deal of ground. In this chapter we will examine some different facets of shielding your wealth against loss. Obviously your aim is to build wealth and build it as quickly as your particular circumstances allow. Once you start acquiring wealth, the last thing you want is see your gains shrink. You want to preserve them so that the growth continues.

The financial principles you have learned thus far from the first three secrets; making it a habit to pay yourself first by saving ten percent of your income, making and following a budget, paying off debt, and starting to invest, are either things you should start doing immediately or start immediately after completing a prerequisite step.

For example, you should start saving and budgeting right away. After saving the first $1,000 to establish an emergency fund, next you should use your ten percent savings to accelerate repayment of all your high interest debt. Then after your debt has been paid off, you should start allocating your ten percent savings to investing for growth. Based on my own experience, I expect that most people should be able to complete all those initial steps within 3 years or so of starting the six secrets system. Certainly the amount of debt a person has will be a factor is determining the time frame. Those with little debt will complete the steps sooner than someone with a lot of debt.

The steps you will take to add the elements to your personal financial plan discussed in this chapter are somewhat different. You aren't expected to complete them immediately but you are urged to finish them at least by the time you start an investing program. That's not to say they are less important than the steps enumerated above because they are vitally important. But while all of the initial steps are aimed at saving you money and starting you on the road to building wealth, the steps involved in the fourth secret are going to cost you money.

Some reading this book may simply not be in the position to spend the money until they have managed to get their personal financial situation off life support and firmly on the road to becoming healthy. Even if you aren't yet in the position to follow the guidance in this chapter, do keep it in mind and follow through as soon as it's financially feasible. These steps become even more important once you have started to accumulate meaningful wealth.

Forewarned is forearmed, so upfront I'll tell you that this will not likely be the most exciting chapter in this book for most people. But it is important stuff. Please don't allow yourself to give in to any temptation to skim over or skip this information. The two primary topics that will be covered in this chapter are estate planning and life insurance.

Estate Planning

Estate planning is simply creating a plan for how a person's wealth will be managed or distributed in the event of incapacitation or death. The first steps involved in estate planning include;

- Making a will.
- Naming a guardian for dependents.
- Naming an executor of the estate to see that the terms of the will are carried out.
- Naming beneficiaries for life insurance and retirement plans.
- Establishing a durable power of attorney.

Estate planning is not a set and forget one-time procedure. Instead it is an ongoing process that requires attention over the course of a person's entire life. Wills have to be updated periodically as one example. In addition a couple of other steps must be added to the above list as a person's asset base increases and if financial goals change. These additional steps include;

- Tax planning to minimize estate taxes.
- Setting up trusts.

While estate planning is a vital and indispensable part of any complete personal financial plan, it is the element of financial planning a great many people ignore. A survey from the legal services website RocketLawyer.com, discovered that "50% of Americans with children do not have a will." Even more disturbing the study revealed that "41% of baby boomers (age 55-64) don't have one."

Let's face it. None of us particularly enjoy contemplating our own mortality. Obviously that is what we are doing when we engage in estate planning. But it must be done. Most of us have people we love who depend us. Being responsible means having a plan in place to take care of them in the event we should become incapacitated or die prematurely.

The tax planning and trust setup considerations typically come later in life once a person has accumulated substantial wealth. Consequently, here we are going to focus only on making a simple will and related tasks.

One of the top three reasons for not having a will, given by respondents in the RocketLawyer.com survey was that they didn't believe they needed a will. What happens when a person dies without a will (or dies intestate in legalese)? Instead of the person's wishes being carried out as happens with a will, the state steps in and assumes responsibility for making all the decisions about the person's estate in accordance with the state's intestacy statute.

Assume a hypothetical young man, married with two children, dies in an automobile accident. While he may have preferred that his entire estate go to his wife if he had drawn a will since his children would later inherit from their mother's estate, the state's intestacy laws might stipulate that his wife get only 60% of his estate and that the remaining 40% be put in trust funds for the children until they reached legal age. That might of course leave the young man's wife in a serious financial bind. She might for example be unable to keep the family home. Or what if he and his partner were living together rather than being married with the two children still in the mix. His partner and mother of his children under the laws of some states would inherit nothing. The entire estate left after creditors had been paid could then be put into trusts for the children once they reached legal age, an even worse situation for her. That's why having a will is so important.

Getting a will prepared does cost money. The cost of having a will prepared by an attorney varies from place to place, but typically a lawyer will prepare a simple will for a few hundred dollars. In comparison to other types of legal services, will preparation is relatively inexpensive since most attorneys will do them for a flat rate rather than billing by the hour. In addition for someone who needs only a simple will, there are several web-based legal services firms where a person can prepare his or her own simple will online for much less than a lawyer would charge.

Regardless of the method chosen the point is everyone, even single people, need a will and should get one prepared at the earliest opportunity. Regardless of the expense, it's simply necessary. And don't forget. As more wealth is accumulated and life changes occur such as marriage, divorce, remarriage, and the birth of children, wills must be updated. Having an out of date will can cause as many problems as not having one. Wills should be reviewed at least annually.

Before leaving the topic of estate planning, we need to look briefly at an associated document, a durable power of attorney which is generally prepared at the same a will is drawn.

A durable power of attorney is a legal document that gives a trusted person the power to act in your behalf if an accident or illness left you unable to make decisions about your medical treatment or the management of your financial affairs. During the length of such incapacitation the person named in the document would be legally permitted to do things like pay your bills, file your taxes, manage your investments, and make medical treatment decisions for you until you are able once again to manage your own affairs. Incapacitation of one spouse or partner could result in severe hardships for the other spouse or partner if no power of attorney existed.

To cover all the bases you likely need two separate documents, one that addresses medical care and the other finances. Like a will, having a durable power of attorney is well worth the time and relatively inexpensive costs required to prepare one.

Having a will and durable power of attorney is an important part of a complete personal financial plan and central to protecting your wealth, the theme of the fourth secret to building wealth. With that, let's move on to the next topic, life insurance.

Life Insurance

Life insurance is another element of having a sound, complete personal financial plan that most people overlook. One would be hard pressed to find someone who doesn't know what life insurance is. It's simply an insurance policy that pays out a sum of money on the death of an insured person, or in some cases after a set period. That said, it would be just about as difficult to find someone who truly understands life insurance. That's understandable given the myriad of choices we are faced with when it comes to buying life insurance. That alone makes life insurance a rather complex matter. Since few people really understand life insurance and even fewer of us enjoy being reminded that we aren't going to live forever, it's simply a subject that people tend to avoid thinking about or doing anything about. As a result, studies tell us that the majority of Americans have too little life insurance and that a great many Americans who should have life insurance don't have any at all. The problem is compounded by the fact that some of us have life insurance when we don't need it and a lot of people have the wrong kind of life insurance.

Let's start with the basics. The purpose of life insurance is to replace the loss of income that would result if an insured person passes away. Life insurance is one thing that we pay for, oftentimes for many years which we will never receive any personal benefit from. By design it is a financial product solely intended to benefit others, the people in our lives that we love and who are dependent on us and our income for financial support. That fact illustrates that there are some people who definitely need to have life insurance but at the same time demonstrates that there are some individuals who don't need to have it. Life insurance is an expense and one we should incur only if it's necessary.

As a general rule, single individuals without dependents do not need life insurance. It's quite like the fact that a person who doesn't own a car doesn't need auto insurance. There is nothing to insure. On the passing of a single person without dependents, his or her estate will generally be sufficient to pay final expenses and to wind up his or her affairs.

Individuals with a spouse or partner and/or children definitely need adequate life insurance. If that describes you, consider how your family's financial circumstances would be affected if you were to die prematurely and your income was taken away. The rent or mortgage payment, debts, monthly bills, and ordinary living expenses would continue to have to be paid. Even if your spouse or partner works full-time, the loss of your income would severely impact their ability to pay all of those things. The reverse is also true. If your spouse or partner passed away, that would have a major impact on your financial circumstances, especially so if you have children. So your spouse or partner also needs life insurance,

Now that we have covered who needs to have life insurance and who doesn't, let's look at some of the options a person has when it comes to buying a life insurance policy. There are quite a number of different types of life insurance.

Basic life insurance is called term life insurance. Term life is the the simplest and generally the least expensive type of life insurance. Term life insurance remains in effect for a specified period of time, typically 10, 20, or 30 years, depending on the option chosen when the policy is purchased or until the insured reaches a specified age. Term life pays the face amount of the policy if the insured person dies within the specified term of the policy, but pays nothing if the insured lives beyond that specified period. Since life insurance rates are based on actuarial calculations used to predict life expectancy, the younger and healthier a person is when buying term life insurance, the cheaper the premiums. Term life insurance is sometimes referred to as temporary insurance to distinguish it from the other major type of life insurance, whole life.

Whole life insurance is offered under a variety of hybrids types including whole or ordinary life insurance, universal life, variable life, and variable-universal life. There are some significant differences among those various types but for our purposes, the main consideration is that whole life in all of its hybrid forms is life insurance with a savings element.

Under limited circumstances, whole life insurance can be an appropriate estate planning tool for some people. Generally however, term life insurance is the best option for the vast majority of people for a number of reasons that we will look at in a moment. But a large percentage of insurance representatives will always start the discussion with a prospective policy buyer by explaining why they should buy a whole life policy in one of its forms.

Certainly some insurance representatives may by virtue of the training they received from their company actually believe that whole life is the superior life insurance product and the best type for people to have. But we can't ignore the fact that the salaries of life insurance representatives are largely commission-based and that representatives make significantly more in commissions selling whole life than they do selling term insurance. That's why as a prospective life insurance policy buyer, you need to understand what kind of life insurance is best suited to your particular needs and circumstances long before you make an appointment with a life insurance salesperson.

Now we can look at the reasons why term life insurance is generally the best option. To begin with, life insurance is something we only need temporarily not permanently. By the time most of us reach a certain age, be it 10, 20, or 30 years down the road, our children will no longer (hopefully at least) be dependent on us for their financial support. Also, over the decades our net worth should grow to the point that our estate would be sufficient to meet the financial support needs of our spouse or partner if we were to pass away. At a point in time, paying insurance premiums would become an unnecessary expense.

Depending on the specific form of whole life insurance a person purchases, the savings component might simply be that a portion of the premium is deposited into a savings account for the benefit of the insured and periodically the insurance company adds a specified amount of interest to the account, paid on the balance. In other types of whole life, the savings component actually is set up almost like a mutual fund investment. Instead of a savings account, the insured selects a type of mutual fund from the options offered by the insurance company. At least in theory, as the fund or funds increases in value over the years so too does the cash value of the policy. At first blush this might sound like a great plan. The truth is however that regardless of how the savings component of a particular whole life policy is set up, the relatively high administrative and maintenance fees charged by the insurance company in connection with the underlying investment make these schemes a poor investment choice for the insured. It's almost always best to buy insurance from an insurance company and to invest your money elsewhere.

Lastly, term life insurance is the most economical type of life insurance to buy. Some individuals pay more in a single month on whole life insurance policy premiums than they would have to pay in an entire year in premiums for a term life policy with the same death benefit or face amount. The rule of thumb is to buy term life and invest the difference elsewhere. Don't allow a life insurance salesperson to sell you the wrong type of life insurance that is going to represent an expense higher than you really should be paying.

If you decide to purchase term life insurance there are some things you need to be aware of. Even in the simplest and most basic type of life insurance policies do differ. For example, depending on the policy terms, premiums may remain level (stay the same) or may increase as you age. That depends on whether you purchase a policy with level premiums or increasing premiums.

Generally with policies that provide for level premiums (premium amount remains the same throughout a specified term) the face amount of the policy, the amount the insurance company would pay to your beneficiaries upon your death, decreases as you age. With increasing premiums, the face amount remains the same over the term of the policy but as you age the premiums are adjusted upwards periodically as established by the terms of the policy.

Let's face it. Insurance companies are in business to make a profit. They can only do that by predicting with reasonable accuracy how long a person is likely to live and charging enough in premiums based on that to earn more than they pay out in benefits. They need enough in income to pay out benefits when they must on the policies they sell and still retain a surplus to provide a profit margin.

A couple of other terms associated with term life insurance you should be aware of are renewable and convertible. Renewable means that you have the option of renewing a life insurance policy upon expiration of the initial term without having to have a medical examination to prove you are in good health. That can be an important consideration if it turns out that you still need life insurance after an initial term is set to expire. As we age our health naturally can at some point start to decline and we are looked at as a bigger risk by insurance companies. Without the option to renew a policy without proving good health, the cost of buying a new life insurance policy might be prohibitively expensive if indeed we could buy life insurance at all.

Convertible term life policies have a conversion provision that permits the policy owner to convert from term life to permanent (whole life) insurance during a specified period of time without having to prove good health. Typically the conversion eligibility period is shorter than the overall term of the policy. Getting a convertible term policy is generally a good idea. Convertible policies are priced competitively in comparison to similar term life policies that don't include this provision so there is nothing to lose. This feature could be a great benefit if there should be some fundamental change in your health or retirement plans during the term of your policy so it's a good option to have and won't cost that much more to get it.

Without knowing the particulars of your specific financial and familial circumstances, I don't presume to advise you on what specific type of life insurance you should purchase. I can only offer the general guidance that individuals with dependents need to include life insurance in their personal financial plan and that renewable, convertible, term life insurance is typically the best type of life insurance to meet the needs of the vast majority of people. Obviously it would take an entire book of its own to tell you everything you might possibly need to know about life insurance and the realist in me tells me that most people wouldn't read such a book anyway. Life insurance is simply not an intriguing enough subject to capture the attention of most people for long. This short explanation of life insurance then certainly won't make anyone an expert on the intricacies of life insurance. But hopefully it will inform those who read it about the major differences between term life and whole life and why one type of life insurance might be preferred over the other.

The information presented should at the very least help you understand the the questions it is important to ask of an insurance salesperson before you agree to purchase a life insurance policy. Questions like these. What is the term of the policy? What benefits would the policy pay out and under what circumstances? How much will the premiums be over the entire term of the policy? Are premiums level or increasing? Does the face value of the policy change over the term of the policy? In the case of term life, is the policy renewable and convertible and if so under what conditions?

The last thing we need to consider about life insurance is this. How much life insurance do we need? This answer to this question is important to make certain we buy enough life insurance to provide sufficient financial security for those who depend on us for financial support. It's equally important to know the answer to that question to make certain that we don't waste money by buying more life insurance than we actually need to accomplish that purpose. This is also something you need to have worked out before shopping for a policy because unscrupulous insurance salespeople, and some do exist, will often push you to buy more insurance than you actually need.

The basic answer to the question of how much life insurance do we need is enough to pay sufficient benefits that when combined with the value of our living estate (all our assets minus all our liabilities) will allow for paying our own final expenses and provide the desired standard of living for our dependents. How much of a policy that amounts to of course varies from person to person and their specific circumstances and financial goals. But here are the specifics you need to consider when deciding how much life insurance to buy.

You need to buy enough life insurance so that when combined with your living estate (excluding non-investment assets like your home or other personal property your spouse or partner would not wish to liquidate if you were to die prematurely), there would be sufficient money to pay your funeral expenses, pay off all debt, pay for future significant expenses such as your children's college expenses, to provide sufficient cash flow to provide for the financial support of your dependents at the desired standard of living, and finally enough to cover inflation. Most people would wish that in the event they died prematurely the standard of living for their family would not suffer as a result. Here I don't want us to get bogged down by making a bunch of complicated financial calculations. Instead I'll simplify it as much as possible. These then are the specifics that go into determining how much life insurance you need:

- How much debt do you owe? You need sufficient life insurance so that the proceeds will pay off all your debts including; mortgage, auto loans, credit cards, student loans, personal loans, etc.

- How much do you earn? Replacing your income is one of the most important purposes of having life insurance. If you want your dependents standard of living to remain the same if you were to die prematurely then you want a policy that will pay out enough to provide an amount that when invested as a lump sum, will yield the equivalent of your annual salary without reducing the principal. Many financial experts recommend that you assume a conservative 8% return on investment.

- How much is the amount of anticipated major future expenses? Paying for your children's college education is the best example here. The cost depends of course on what type of college education you envision providing your kids whether it is paying for a degree from a private or public university. A recent study says that the average cost of a four-year degree by 2018 will be around $115,000, not including things like room and board. That figure could be reduced by things like attending an in-state public university, part-time work during college, financial aid, and scholarships, but you may want to have sufficient insurance so that the proceeds would provide for the bulk of it.

- How much would your living estate contribute to the above? Here we are talking about specific assets such as the amount of money you have in savings, investments, and personal assets that your spouse might choose to liquidate. Things like a boat, extra car, vacation property, etc.

Answering the above question determines how much life insurance you need. Let's consider an example. A hypothetical family, Tom and his wife Julie have a mortgage of $130,000 and other debts of $9,000. Tom earns $50,000 per year. He and his wife have two children. Tom and Julie have $5,000 in a savings account. Tom has $28,000 in his 401k at work and the family has $18,000 in taxable investment accounts. Both Tom and Julie have cars. Tom's car has a resale value of $11,000 and would not be needed if he were to die prematurely. Tom's life insurance requirement then would be calculated as follows;

1. Debts: $139,000

2. Income replacement: $417,000

3. Future large expenses (kid's college): $200,000 (Tom's projections)

4. Less: Value of Tom's living estate: $62,000

Tom needs about $694,000 in life insurance ($139,000 + $417,000 + $200,000) - $62,000.

When calculating how much life insurance you should buy, also remember to deduct any life insurance coverage you already have. Perhaps you already have some life insurance through your employer. Sometimes people have life insurance through a lender that will pay off the balance of a debt if the debtor should die. Those who serve in the military reserves or National Guard also have Service members Group Life Insurance (SGLI). For military reservists SGLI also reduces the amount of life insurance a person needs to buy.

To summarize, estate planning and life insurance are the focus of the fourth secret to building wealth and both are essential to protecting your wealth from loss. They are also two vital elements of the comprehensive, complete personal financial plan that the six secrets to building wealth can help you achieve.

6

Fifth Secret: Buying a Home is Still the Best Investment

Obviously many people these days, even many financial experts would disagree with the premise of this chapter, that buying a home is still the best investment. But based on my own experience as well as that of many of the people I know personally, I still say without any reservations that from an individual perspective, the best investment you can make is buying the primary residence you live in. This is definitely a real estate investment that most people should make.

It's easy to find articles in financial magazines and on financial websites these days that tell you buying a home is no longer a smart decision, but I beg to differ. I think much of the anti-home buying sentiment stems from the housing market crash in 2008. Yes, home prices plummeted and many people lost their homes to foreclosure. But to large extent that occurred as a result of irresponsible sub-prime lending practices followed by many mortgage lenders which was in truth encouraged by the federal government. I think think the further we get from the housing market melt-down, the more our society will again embrace home ownership in favor of renting. Owning a home I think is still an indispensable part of of achieving the American dream.

Buying a house is not necessarily an investment in the sense that everyone intends to sell their home and cash in on the price appreciation that occurs over time. Some do. Some people downsize when they retire. They sell the large home where they raised their family and use the sale proceeds to buy a smaller, less expensive home. They bank or invest the rest to supplement their retirement savings. Also, people often buy a modest starter home as their first residence and later after it has appreciated in value they sell it and use the profits to step up to a larger and newer home that better fits their needs.

There are still many advantages of owning your own home over renting. For one thing, rents are quite pricey these days, particularly in certain markets. I live well outside a major market area but rent is very expensive where I presently live and I'm glad I'm not a renter for that reason. In many parts of the country mortgage payments are significantly less than rent payments. Rent payments can rise every time a lease comes up for renewal while a fixed rate monthly mortgage payment remains the same for as many as 30 years.

To be sure there are costs associated with owning your own home that you don't have to pay when renting. Things like property taxes, home insurance, repairs, and maintenance. Still owning seems like the better deal given that housing values during normal economic times increase, roughly at the same rate as inflation. I don't subscribe to the idea that renting is just throwing away money. You do receive value, a place to live, when renting. But clearly at the end of the day you don't have anything to show for months or years of paying rent.

The way that buying a home helps you to build wealth is that owning a home relatively rapidly makes a very large contribution to your net worth. At first, when you buy a home even though you add a substantial asset to your net worth calculation, the value of that asset is mostly offset by the corresponding liability, a 20 or 30 year mortgage. But every month when you make your mortgage payment, the liability decreases while your home is appreciating in value. Even before your mortgage is paid off, after a number of years the value of your home as an asset far surpasses the liability of your mortgage balance and your home significantly and positively impacts on your total net worth, another term for your wealth. If you accelerate the repayment of mortgage, the impact is even more significant.

I rented for many years but I now own my home and have no mortgage. My monthly housing expenses, which consist only of utility costs, property taxes, and routine maintenance, average just a few hundred dollars per month. That's enormously cheaper than paying rent in my area or anywhere else I might choose to live. That frees up a lot of discretionary income that I'm able to invest for growth that I wouldn't have otherwise.

When it makes sense to rent instead of owning

Despite my conviction that buying a home is usually the wiser financial decision, admittedly there are circumstances where it makes more sense to rent. Our society is far more mobile today than in times past when owning a home has been viewed as the way to go. Some people for example have jobs where their employer requires them to move relatively frequently, at least every three years or so. According to experts, it takes about five years for your investment in a home to start earning you money. That being true, buying a home would not be a good decision for those who know they would be relocating in 5 years or less. You have to stay in a home long enough to build the necessary equity to offset the costs of making a down payment, paying closing costs, and real estate commissions when selling.

Those in unstable relationships also are better advised to rent. Owning a house with someone whom you may end up divorcing or breaking up with simply adds more problems you don't need to an already difficult situation. That's one concern at least that single home buyers don't have to deal with.

Are you a free spirit who loves flexibility and having the choice to relocate on the spur of the moment over being tie down to one geographic location for years and years. If so, buying a house wouldn't be a good financial decision. You are better off renting where at worst you are only tied to a location for the duration of a twelve-month lease.

If you want to own your own home but haven't saved enough for a 20% down payment, it's wiser to continue renting until you have. Even after the 2008 debacle, there remain ways to buy a house and get a mortgage without paying 20% down, but it's not a smart move.

For one thing, you will be hit with private mortgage insurance premiums (PMI) which will tack an additional hundred dollars or more to your monthly mortgage payment until your achieve a 78% equity stake. In addition buying without at least 20% down puts you in a precarious financial situation. You're mortgage payments will be higher and that generally will result in your total housing expenses consuming more of your income than they should. Buying a house too soon, or more house than you can afford is a quick trip down the lane to living paycheck to paycheck.

There are a few other reasons where I think a person would be better off renting than buying a house but those above are the main ones. Generally speaking, if you have put down roots and don't anticipate relocating in the next five years if ever, are single or in a stable relationship, and you have the savings to comfortably pay 20% down, purely from a financial perspective you are far better off buying a home over paying rent. Making your home a profitable investment is a tried and true method of building wealth.

7

Sixth Secret: Assure Your Future Wealth

We've arrived at the sixth and final secret to building wealth. The previous five secrets contain principles that should of course be permanently incorporated into your financial plan. However, many of those initial principles will also yield some short-term, immediate positive results. Now it's time to look to the future and at principles that aim to produce long-term results.

Most people will find a way to start saving ten percent of their income quickly. Many will achieve the $1,000 emergency fund savings goal in a year or less. Paying off debt may take longer, but again depending on how much work and effort a person can and is willing to put into it, most people can get rid of all their high interest debt within three years. Recently I read an article about a couple with a combined annual income of $67,000 who managed to pay off nearly $120,000 in debt in just under four years. So getting rid of debt is certainly possible. People have paid off some staggering amounts of debt in some amazingly short periods of time once they committed to a plan.

But now it's time to turn our attention to the long game portion of creating a complete, wealth-building personal financial plan, assuring your future wealth. Earlier in the book I promised that we would get to a discussion on retirement and that's the subject of this chapter.

Saving for retirement at the right time

According to the latest Retirement Confidence Survey from the Employee Benefit Research Institute (EBRI), many Americans are falling woefully short of saving enough for retirement. While the Federal Reserve recently indicated that the average American has about $60,000 in savings for retirement that is a median figure and more than a little misleading. The EBRI's study paints a much more realistic picture, reporting that; only 14% of Americans have more than $250,000 saved for retirement, an eye-popping 64% have less than $50,000 in retirement savings, and that about 25% have less than $1,000 in earmarked for retirement.

Given the EBRI data, doing your best to max out annual contributions to your 401k or IRA is a worthy goal. However as I stated previously, there are people today living paycheck to paycheck because they are doing that very thing. They simply aren't in the financial circumstances that allow them to afford devoting so much of their income to retirement savings. They have missed a few steps in their financial planning that needs to be addressed before retirement savings.

Saving for retirement is necessary and clearly most Americans aren't saving enough, but that can't become so much of a focus that it results in people not having an emergency fund, not saving and investing for the present, and making minimum payments on high interest debt. Those are the things that keep people broke and living paycheck to paycheck. Once an emergency fund has been established, high interest debts have been paid off, and you're investing for future growth, then it's time to turn you attention to retirement saving.

Right about now some reading this book might be wondering about the ten percent fund. Didn't I say that if you did nothing else but make it a habit to save and invest ten percent of your income you would someday be wealthy, perhaps wealthier than you ever dreamed of? Yes, I did say that and I'm not retracting that. But the ten percent savings is not part of retirement planning or retirement savings. Think of the ten percent savings as the "I finally have wealth" money. It's the money that will finally allow you to feel what being financially free is supposed to be all about. It is the money that will allow you to acquire some of the luxuries of life without feeling guilty about it and especially without having to go into debt to get them. Retirement savings is a completely separate savings category all its own. Trust me on this. If you commit to the six secrets to building wealth and follow the underlying principles, you will be able to afford to save ten percent of your income for wealth building and still save what you should for retirement on top of it.

How much to save for retirement

How much should you sock away in retirement savings? Ask any financial expert and you will likely get a different answer. A common figure often heard however is 20% of your income and that meets my personal reasonableness test. For most people, that should be enough over 20, 25, or 30 years to grow into a nest egg large enough to meet his or her retirement needs. I won't give a specific total figure to aim at. I find it ridiculous when some so-called experts tell us you have to have $1 million or more in your retirement account by the time you retire to have a secure retirement. Circumstances vary too much from person to person. Some may earn enough that they can easily accumulate $1 million. Others can only dream of that. Why set people up for failure? Such nonsense, while perhaps well-meaning may actually serve to demotivate some from saving at all.

Making your retirement plan

Social Security I feel is one thing that causes people to procrastinate when it comes to saving for their own retirement. In the back of their minds is that no matter what social security will be there for them. It's not like they are going to be homeless or go hungry even if they don't manage to save much on their own. There is a grain of truth to that. Social Security has its problems. The last five Trustees Reports have all indicated that the Social Security's Old-Age, Survivors, and Disability Insurance (OASDI) Trust Fund reserves will become depleted sometime between 2033 and 2036 under the set of economic and demographic assumptions used in making those predictions. The future of Social Security looks gloomy, but a cursory look at the history of the system will show that is nothing new.

Could Social Security become and insolvent and stop paying benefits? Yes, theoretically just about anything is possible. But I don't believe that will ever happen. I don't even believe things will ever get to the point that the social security payments to current retirees will be cut, which is actually more of possibility than the payments stopping altogether. The reason I believe this is because I have faith in our politicians and political system.

You see, we the people, mostly out of apathy have allowed our federal representative government to become populated by a professional politician class. Our representatives, to use the term loosely, in the US Congress really care about only one thing, getting reelected again and again and retaining their perk-filled positions in the US Senate and House of Representatives. It's a great gig, comes with many advantages, and is evidently quite financially rewarding given the number of present and past congressional members that were of modest means when first elected but are now worth millions. Simply suggesting that social security be tampered with even in the slightest way creates a firestorm of rage and anger from the citizenry. Allowing the Social Security system to actually fail would be nothing short of political suicide for every politician in the government. They will hem and haw, debate and staff useless committees to study the problem, and procrastinate until the final hour. But at the last moment, our representatives will act. They will cobble a bill together, kick the can a little further down the road, but do something that keeps the good old Social Security Trust Fund solvent for another couple of decades or so.

The point is, ignore the gloom and doom crowd who ring their hands and proclaim that Social Security will go broke and cease to exist. If that should ever happen, our country will literally be in such a horrific situation that a failed social security system will be the last thing any of us will be worried about. You know something like Armageddon.

You can and should consider social security benefits as one of pillars of your retirement plan. Just recognize that social security benefits is only a part of and not the sum of your retirement plan. Presently the average retiree is receiving about $1,340 in monthly benefits. That's sufficient to meet quite a bit of a retiree's basic financial needs. But that's the point. Who really wants to live at a bare sustenance level in retirement?

Not to mention, folks are living longer these days. Each year, the government using the current version of voodoo economics proclaims there has been no inflation. So in most years, social security recipients do not receive a cost of living increase while their private pension receiving peers do. Huh? How does that happen? But I digress. After 10 or 20 years of "no inflation" government Jedi mind tricks $1,340 is not going to go nearly as far towards meeting those basic expenses as it once did.

We must also take into consideration that Medicare premiums, deducted right off the top of every social security check keep increasing and a lot. What should really fill us full of dread is the possibility that the day may dawn when there is nothing left from our social security checks after our Medicare premiums are deducted. Those sky rocketing premiums is another little thing the government forgot to mention while selling us on the illusion of universal access to health care, the Ponzi scheme better known at the Patient Protection and Affordable Care Act.

The takeaway here is do include future social security payments in your retirement planning, just view it as what it is, a retirement supplement. Nothing else, nothing more. You have to save for your own retirement and you need to start as soon as you have achieved the other priority milestones we've discussed that must come first.

Where to save for retirement

We have a good many choices when it comes to where to invest our retirement savings. If you have it available where you work, the 401k is your first and best option for two reasons. First, 401k contributions are tax deferred meaning that the amount withheld from your paychecks for income taxes is actually reduced when you participate in a 401k at work. In addition many employers match employee contributions up to a certain percentage of eligible compensation. As an example, my current employer matches employee contributions dollar for dollar up to the first 3% of compensation contributions, 50 cents on the dollar of the next 2%, and 25 cents on the dollar of the next 1% of compensation contributions. Consequently, those who do not take full advantage of employer matches by participating in their company's 401k and contributing at least enough to capture the maximum employer match are literally turning down free retirement money.

In 2016 most individuals are allowed to contribute up to $18,000 to his or her 401k. There are catch up provisions for older workers. Most of us working stiffs are never going to approach that lofty threshold with our 20% savings plan. But that's okay. We will just have to accept that private jets, regular holidays on the French Riviera, and gambling at Monte Carlo are not going to be a part of our retirement future. We can only do what we can do. If a person has a 401k that offers decent investing options and reasonable fees, he or she may decide to simply contribute the entire 20% to his or her 401k. But there also exists an option to contribute only up to the percentage that captures the full employer match and to then turn to better options for the remainder of your 20% retirement savings. But before we have that discussion, we need to look at an option for those who do not work for an employer offering a 401k

The venerable traditional IRA

Absent the potential employer contribution matches offered by 401k plans, the old school traditional IRA still offers one way to capture a tax benefit for those who don't have access to an employer sponsored retirement plan. You can open an IRA at virtually any financial institution these days including mutual fund companies and stock brokers. For 2016 up to $5,500 ($6,500 if you're age 50 or older) can be contributed to a traditional IRA and the full amount contributed is tax deductible if you (and your spouse, if you are married) aren't covered by a retirement plan at work. As with all things IRS, especially for married folks there are some complexities involved so either review IRS Publication 590-A, Contributions to Individual Retirement Arrangements (IRAs) for complete details, or consult a tax professional before deciding whether to open and contribute to a traditional IRA.

Roth IRAs

Anyone, even those who do have access to a 401k or other employer sponsored retirement plan and participate in the plan has the option to open and contribute to a Roth IRA. The Roth IRA in my opinion definitely deserves a spot on the all-time greatest thing since sliced bread list.

Single workers earning less than $117,000 and married workers filing joint tax returns earning less than $184,000 can contribute up to $5,500 ($6,500 if you're age 50 or older) to a Roth IRA. Roth IRA contributions are after-tax contributions and aren't tax deductible, but do offer something even better. Those who satisfy all IRS requirements can receive tax-free distributions from a Roth IRA as long as contributions have been made for a minimum of 5 years beginning with the first tax year a Roth IRA was set up and distributions are taken after reaching age 59½ or after becoming disabled. Another great feature of Roth IRAs is unlike traditional IRAs there are no mandatory distributions when reaching a specified age. You can leave your money in a Roth IRA for life if you choose.

As indicated earlier, some with 401k plan access may find it makes sense to contribute to a 401k until the maximum employer match is captured and to then contribute the remainder of their retirement savings to a Roth IRA. Since you can open a Roth IRA at virtually any financial institution, opening one with your broker or mutual fund company can allow you to invest in some much more superior asset classes than you may find available within your company 401k plan.

Again, review IRS Publication 590-A, Contributions to Individual Retirement Arrangements (IRAs) for complete details, or consult a tax professional before deciding whether to open and contribute to a Roth IRA.

There are other choices when it comes to places to save and invest retirement savings. Employees of municipal and state governments for example have access to plans that are similar to 401k plans but in my opinion inferior. Federal employees also have their own retirement plan. There are retirement annuities available, which in my considered opinion are best avoided by most people because they lack flexibility and the expenses charged by institutions offering them are generally prohibitive.

The options that have been discussed at length here are usually the best options for most individuals. But you are encouraged to get a book devoted entirely to the discussion of retirement plans and strategies if you wish to explore all the possibilities. The information in such books is far more comprehensive and complete than can be covered here in a single chapter.

The least you need to know about the sixth secret to wealth and assuring your future wealth is that you do need to save for your own retirement. You should save and invest your retirement money using the most advantageous plan available and the ones that you feel most comfortable with.

In concluding this chapter, I think it important to note one last thing. It isn't foolish or irresponsible to take on some reasonable risk when it comes to saving for retirement when you are in your twenties and early thirties in pursuit of potentially higher returns. However, your overall strategy must be more conservative than one you might follow when investing your ten percent savings in taxable accounts. Time is the most valuable commodity when it comes to long-term investing which is what retirement saving truly is. If you're older and playing catch up, you don't have the luxury of absorbing losses because you don't have time on your side to recover from losses. You by necessity must be more risk averse and more selective in what asset classes you choose to invest your retirement savings in. For you, capital preservation rather than pursuit of potentially exceptional growth is the order of the day.

That concludes the revelation of the six secrets to building wealth. Please continue to the next chapter where we endeavor to put the secrets all together within the framework of a complete, wealth-building personal financial plan.

8

Putting It All Together

We have covered a lot of territory in this book. All six secrets to building wealth have been revealed. Hopefully each of the precepts have been explained with sufficient clarity to empower people to use them, grasp the significance of each one, and understand how all six fit together to form a complete, powerful, unified personal financial plan.

"Simple is as simple does"

Nothing in this book is particularly complicated, hard to comprehend, or master. Anyone can learn these powerful financial principles and start using them immediately to improve their financial circumstances. All that is required are some fifth grade math skills and a commitment to take some simple, relatively pain-free steps to get started on the road to financial independence.

Some may even be bothered by the very simplicity of these six secrets. How could a set of guidelines so simple and easy to use help anyone escape living paycheck to paycheck and start building real wealth? As the old saying goes, simple things confound the wise. Oftentimes it's the simple things that trip us up. The real power of these principles of personal money management is found in their simplicity. They are to large extent just plain, old-fashioned, common sense money management. These principles will work for anyone regardless of income level. A modest income is not an obstacle to gaining the benefits of following the financial roadmap presented in this book. Those willing to make a commitment to follow a handful of easy, painless steps, will gradually build wealth and see their financial circumstances improve substantially.

Understanding basic personal finance concepts enables you to make informed decisions about your personal finances. One of the primary goals behind this book was empowering people to do exactly that. I'm passionate about promoting financial literacy.

The six secrets to building wealth represent a blueprint for constructing your own complete, comprehensive, wealth-building personal financial plan. Within the six secrets you will find all six elements of a complete financial plan that most financial experts advocate;

- Budgeting
- Money management and credit management
- Plan for Investing
- Plan for protecting your wealth
- Plan for retirement
- Estate planning

This book covers them all but presents them in a particular order. I believe from experience that it is important. Have you ever tried to assembly something without bothering with reading and following the instructions only to end up with a frustrating mess? The six secrets works the same way. I think it is essential to follow the steps outlined in this book in a particular sequence to get the most from them. Here as a refresher is a summary of those steps;

- Establish the habit of paying yourself first by saving the first 10% of your income every pay period.

- Create a budget and learn to follow it. You have to have a plan to gain complete control over your spending. Not having a plan is a plan. It's a plan to fail.

- Use the 10% savings first to establish a $1,000 emergency fund deposited in a savings account.

- After establishing an emergency fund, use the 10% savings to accelerate repayment of all high interest debt until all of it is paid off.

- After becoming debt free (except for mortgages), invest the 10% savings for future growth.

- Once you start building wealth, protect it with estate planning and adequate life insurance.

- Unless you have a compelling reason not to, make your home a profitable investment by buying and owning your primary residence instead of being a renter.

- Save 20% of your income towards retirement to assure your future wealth.

Follow the guideposts

Until you have an emergency fund, are debt-free (excluding a mortgage), and are investing your ten percent savings for future growth, it's important not to deviate from the order above. There is often the temptation to try and do too much at once. For example, some might feel tempted to start paying off debt before achieving a $1,000 emergency fund balance. Others may get impatient and decide to start an investing program before they finish paying off all high interest debt. Don't do it. Avoid the temptation. Remain patient. Skipping steps or trying to do two incompatible things at once is counterproductive and will only slow your progress towards achieving your ultimate goals.

Once you have completed the first basic steps however, the later steps do lend themselves to being worked on concurrently. You may for example work on the step aimed at protecting your wealth while buying a home. You don't of course have to pay off your mortgage before you start saving for retirement. The later steps are more compatible with being taken simultaneously. Part of the reason for that is your overall financial circumstances will be vastly improved by the time you reach those last steps on the list, assuming you accomplished the basics ones first.

A request

Thank you for reading this book. I hope that you find the six secrets to building wealth as powerful and effective as I did when I first discovered them and started using them. I'd very much appreciate it if you would consider posting a review of this book at the retail site where you purchased it. Of course I hope you found the book useful and will post a favorable review. But that isn't the motivation behind my request. I ask only that you post an honest review for the benefit of others who may consider reading this book, whether your opinions are favorable or otherwise.

In addition I'd love to hear your story. If you put these six secrets to work and find they help you to escape living paycheck to paycheck and to start building wealth, I invite you to write me at larrydarter@thesixsecrets.com to share your experiences. With your permission of course, I'd love to feature your story on my website as an encouragement to others.

Parting thought

I encourage you to continue learning and building your personal finance skill set. This book is just a first step. There are many more excellent books available that focus exclusively on each of the elements that make up a complete and effective personal financial plan. In particular I recommend that you read and study books on investing and investment strategies. The more you learn about investing, the easier it will become to tap into the wealth-building potential of the markets.

To borrow a line from Morpheus of Matrix fame, "I can only show you the door. You're the one that has to walk through it." You can put this book down and do nothing with what I've shared and the story ends. You can return to life as usual, living paycheck to paycheck, worrying whether this is the month when you won't be able to make ends meet. Or you can act on what you've learned, start being proactive, and put these wealth-building principles to work. But if you choose that path, don't procrastinate. Start taking the steps immediately. Start your ten percent savings program, create a budget, and one by one continue with the steps until you've achieved your financial goals. Starting early allows you to leverage time to your advantage, making it an ally. Procrastination on the other hand makes time your enemy. To illustrate that allow me to leave you with this story.

Doug worked part-time throughout his high school years. His parents had always encouraged him to save part of his earnings. Doug started saving $1,000 a year starting when he was 15. Doug's father spent a lot of time watching investment programs on television so Doug knew a little about the stock market. Instead of just depositing his savings in a savings account, Doug decided to invest his savings in the stock market. After high school, Doug continued working part-time during college and after graduation found a full-time job. For 10 years Doug continued investing his $1,000 in the stock market, earning an average of 12% per year on his investments. After 10 years, Doug met a girl and got married. Soon Doug, Jr. was on the way. Doug stopped adding money to his investments when the bills and expenses started taking every dollar he earned. But to his credit, Doug left his investment in the market untouched.

Compare Doug's story to that of his twin brother Dave. The two couldn't have been more different when it came to their approach to finances. Dave liked to have fun. While he worked part-time during high school and college too, he ignored the advice of his parents and never saved a dime. He spent every cent he earned from those early paychecks on youthful indiscretions in pursuit of the good times. It wasn't until Dave turned 40 that he finally saw the light, woke up, and realized he would have nothing but Social Security to retire on if he didn't start saving. Dave became a changed man and started saving with a vengeance, socking away $10,000 every year for the next 25 years until he retired.

Who had more money at age 65? Intuitively one would think it was Dave. After all he saved a lot more per year and for more than twice as many years as his brother Doug. If your guess is Doug actually had more money at 65, it's probably only because you sensed a setup, didn't you? Clever aren't you? But yes, if you guessed Doug, you're correct. His 10 years of saving $1,000 per year, $10,000 in total and the same amount his brother Dave saved every year for 25 years, netted him $1.8 million by age 65. Dave on the other hand scrimped and pinched pennies for 25 years to save $250,000 which he invested at the same 12% average rate of return as Doug earned. Still he ended up with just under $1.5 million at age 65. Neither will starve during retirement, but you should see the point made about the importance of time. Doug's money grew for 50 years, twice as long as Dave's and that made all the difference.

Learn more

As a bonus for buying and reading this book, you can find The Six Secrets on the web. We have created a companion site to the book that you can access at www.thesixsecrets.com. When you visit the website you can sign up for our free monthly newsletter, find tips and more information on each of the six secrets, and resources to help build a solid investment strategy. We hope you will visit the site, bookmark it, and return again and again.

www.ingramcontent.com/pod-product-compliance
Lightning Source LLC
LaVergne TN
LVHW051755250225
804528LV00002B/299